R. Tate

The Gastropods of the Older Tertiary of Australia

R. Tate

The Gastropods of the Older Tertiary of Australia

ISBN/EAN: 9783337851613

Printed in Europe, USA, Canada, Australia, Japan

Cover: Foto ©Andreas Hilbeck / pixelio.de

More available books at **www.hansebooks.com**

The Gastropods of the Older Tertiary of Australia.

Part IV. (including Supplement to Part III.).

By Professor Ralph Tate.

[Read October 17, 1893.]

Plates VI.–X.

FAMILY CYPRÆIDÆ.

Cypræa Mulderi, *Tate.*

(Trans. Roy. Soc. S. Aust., vol. XIII., 1892, pl. ix., f. 4 : without description.)

Shell depressedly globose, spire concealed ; basal outline oblong ; back almost circular in basal outline, polished, marked with circular contusions varying from 4 to 5 mm. in diameter. Anterior canal abruptly upturned, flanked on each side by a broadly-triangular, slightly concave, thickened extension of the base. Posterior canal short, with very wide flanges, the left one more extended than the right. Base nearly flat, much thickened : outer lip excessively inflected, rounded, its inner margin set with nearly equal and somewhat slender rounded ridges ; inner lip with a broad convex area steeply sloping inwards, the anterior-third furnished with about seven ridges narrower than the intervening sulcations, the rest of the lip edentulous.

Dimensions.—Total length, 100 mm.: width, 64 mm.; height, 50 mm.: length of back, 66 mm.

Localities.—Eocene ; in a well-sinking at Belmont, near Geelong, one example, collected and presented by Mr. Mulder, to whom the species is dedicated : Bellarine Peninsula (Hall and Pritchard).

Affinity.—This species comes near to *C. platypyga*, McCoy, but the back is not pyriform, the anterior canal much reflected, and the shape of the base and details of the aperture are different ; otherwise it might be regarded as a senile form of that species.

Subgenus Cypræedia, *Swainson*, 1840.

Dorsal surface with revolving threads or tessellated ornament. Distinguished from *Cypræovula*, Gray, 1824, by the absence of a posterior apertural notch. One living species, *C. cancellata*, is known, and there are five in the European Eocene.

Cypræadia clathrata, *Tate.*

(Trans. Roy. Soc. S. Aust., vol. XIII., 1892, pl. ix., fig. 1 ; without description.)

Shell oval-pyriform ; anterior canal produced and somewhat dilated at the end. The surface is ornamented by revolving slender threads, alternately large and small, which are crossed by transverse threads equal in strength to the longitudinal secondaries ; the intersections of the two sets of threads produce rectangular interspaces, which are very finely reticulate-striate. There are about ten primary revolving threads in about the middle-third of the dorsal surface, equal to 8 mm. of the axial length.

Dimensions.—Length, 27 mm.; width, 18 mm.

Locality.—Eocene marls, Blanche Point, Aldinga Bay. This species resembles *C. elegans*, Defr., but the pits between the primary threads are oblong, not square ; the interstitial ornament is finely reticulate ; and the canal is more produced and dilated.

FAMILY SCALARIIDÆ.

Crossea semiornata, *spec. nov.* Pl. x., fig. 10.

Shell depressedly conoidal, of four whorls : the first two convex.

The penultimate whorl is quadrate in section, ornamented with an elevated rounded carina at the shoulder, a similar one mid-way to the anterior suture, and a threadlet margining each suture, which is sub-canaliculate ; the whole surface crossed by stout equidistant riblets, which are approximately axial on the anterior-half of the whorls, and produce rectangular pits between the revolving cinguli, on the posterior-half the riblets are oblique. The body-whorl is convex, interrupted in the posterior-third by a slight keel continuous with the posterior cinguli of the penultimate whorl ; the ornament of the penultimate is continued on to the body-whorl, but gradually fades away at about a-half turn, the rest of the surface being polished and obscurely striated coincident with the outer lip.

Dimensions.—Length and width, 2 mm. (vix).

Locality.—Eocene ; Bird-rock Bluff, Spring Creek, near Geelong (two exs.).

In my synopsis of the species (living and fossil) of this genus, *C. semiornata* will belong to section 2 of "group III." from the other members of which it is distinguishable by its fenestrated ornament and smooth body-whorl.

Scalaria (Acrilla) leptalea, *spec. nov.* Pl. x., fig. 1.

Shell thin, very slender, imperforated : ordinary whorls, six, convex, slightly angulated post-medially ; nuclear whorls two and a-half, smooth and polished, the anterior one angulated posteriorly, the next is slightly inflated ending in a bulbiform tip.

The posterior spire-whorls are distantly costated, the others are ornamented with curved lamelliform costæ, separated by little wider intervals.

Base of body-whorl flatly-rounded, smooth, angulated at the periphery ; the peripheral keel crenulated ; aperture oval, the major diameter axial.

Dimensions.—Length, 4 ; breadth, ·5.

Locality.—Eocene ; Bullin Merri, near Camperdown (one ex.).

The nearest ally of this new species is *S. crebrelamellata*, from which it differs by its more slender shape, less crowded lamellæ, and the absence of spiral ornament on the base as well as on the whorls ; the apex is also different, and the whorls are not so flat.

FAMILY NATICID.E.

GENUS NATICA.

SYNOPSIS OF SPECIES.

Umbilicus with a funiculus, without posterior callosity (NATICA, s.s.).

    Shell thin, whorls slightly tabulated, funicular expansion thinly everted.   1.   *Hamiltonensis.*

    Shell solid, whorls regularly convex, funicular expansion stout.   2.   *subNoæ.*

Umbilicus more or less filled with a funicular callosity confluent with the columella-border (NEVERITA).

    Umbilicus filled with a callosity; shell hemisphæric.   3.   *gibbosa.*

    Umbilicus almost concealed by posterior callosity; shell oblong-oval.   4.   *cixumbilicata.*

Umbilicus distinctly funiculate.

    Shell narrow-oval, spire produced.

        Length more than 2 x width, an antesutural band.   5.   *balteatella.*

        Length less than 2 x width, no sutural band.   6.   *subvarians.*

    Shell broadly oval, spire very short ; body-whorl medially depressed.   7.   *varians.*

    Shell globose-conic, whorls ventricose ; spire elevated.   8.   *Wintlei.*

Umbilicus not distinctly funiculate.

    Shell globose, spire prominent.   9.   *Mooraboolensis.*

    Shell hemisphæric, spire almost concealed.   10.   *substolida.*

Umbilicus simple, open : shell globulose (NATICINA).
Surface sculptured.
    Surface grooved ; shell solid.   11.   *arata*.
    Ornament of spiral wavy threads : shell thin.
        12.   *limata*.
Surface smooth, or nearly so.
    Suture canaliculate, umbilicus small, not margined.
        13.   *polita*.
    Suture impressed : umbilicus wide, margined ; body-
    whorl inflated.   14.   *perspectiva*.
    Suture linear ; umbilicus small, not margined.
        15.   *Aldingensis*.
Umbilicus simple, very large : shell depressed, auriform
    (SIGARETOPSIS).   16. *subinfundibulum*.

1. Natica Hamiltonensis, *Tate.* Pl. x., fig. 6.

N. Wintlei, var. *Hamiltonensis*, Tenison-Woods, Proc. Lin. Soc., N.S.W., vol. III., p. 229, tab. 21, fig. 8, 1878.

Shell globulose, fragile ; spire short ; whorls four and a-half, of very rapid increase, smooth or faintly wrinkled around suture : apical whorl flat, the others rotund, more abruptly sloping to the posterior suture ; suture linear.

Aperture broadly oval, slightly oblique, outer and basal margins acute : columella slightly arched, thin, joined to the outer lip by a thin callus : umbilicus narrow, with a not very prominent funiculus, which is defined in front by a narrow groove, but the umbilicus is broader and deep behind it.

Dimensions of a large specimen :—Length, 20 ; width, 19 : vertical height of aperture, 15 : radius of aperture, 11 : width of umbilicus, 2.

Localities. –EOCENE—Muddy Creek (very common) !: Mornington !: Bird-rock Bluff (rare) !: Cheltenham !: Gellibrand River !; Fyansford !; Turritella-beds, Aldinga Cliffs and Adelaide-bore !: River Murray Cliffs ! MIOCENE—Kalima, Gippsland Lakes (rare) !

Remarks.—Tenison-Woods was acquainted with only immature examples (about 4 mm. diameter) of this species, which he referred under a varietal name to his *N. Wintlei.* In the adult stage, such as I have illustrated, the differences indicated between it and *N. Wintlei* are more accentuated. *N. Hamiltonensis* is a fragile shell, with a shorter spire and more convex whorls, whilst the absence of a callus on the posterior part of the columella is a very conspicuous feature.

Among living species with which I have compared it, it makes the nearest approach to *N. Zealandica*, Q. & G., but differs by more inflated spire-whorls and slender funiculus.

2. Natica subNoæ, *spec. nov.* Pl. vi., fig. 1.

Shell solid, smooth, shining, hemisphæric; whorls four and a-half, transversely finely-lined; suture concealed.

Aperture obliquely lunate, outer lip acute; columella nearly vertical; umbilicus wide, a funiculus in the anterior-third, narrow but elevated, terminating in a moderately large oval callosity, confluent in front with the columella, but separated above by a notch, beyond which the columella spreads slightly to join the outer lip.

Shelly opercula occur in association with this species at Spring Creek, which are very similar to those of such species of *Natica* (s.s.) as *N. millepunctata*.

Dimensions.—Length, 11 : breadth, 10 ; length of columella, 8 ; width of aperture, 5 ; width of umbilicus, 2·55.

Localities. — EOCENE : Bird-rock Bluff ! ; Muddy Creek ! ; Birregurra *(Mulder)* ! ; Table Cape ! ; Camperdown !.

Affinities.—This new species has a considerable resemblance to *N. Noæ*, D'Orb., *N. hemipleres*, Cossmann, and other allied species of the Parisian Eocene. From both it differs by concealment of the suture. In shape it is more like *N. hemipleres*, but its apical whorls are flatter. From *N. Noæ* it is distinguished by narrower shape, more oblique aperture, and stouter funicular dilatation more anteriorly situated.

3. Natica gibbosa, *Hutton.* Pl. vi., fig. 4.

Reference.—Trans. N. Zealand Inst., vol. XVIII., p. 334, 1886.

"Shell large, solid, smooth, gibbous, the spire almost buried ; the body-whorl gibbous posteriorly. Aperture semicircular, the columella callus very large, filling the posterior portion of the aperture, and eventually covering the whole umbilical region."

Dimensions.—Length, 39 ; breadth, 37 ; diameter and radius of aperture, 34, 16·5.

Locality not actually known, but reported "a well-sinking in the Murray Desert;" the age is doubtfully Miocene.

Professor Hutton records the species from the Pareora system of New Zealand, and one occurrence from that of Wanganui.

4. Natica vixumbilicata, *Tenison-Woods.* Pl. x., fig. 9.

Reference.—Proc. Roy. Soc., Tasmania, for 1876, p. 111 (1877).

Synonym.—*N. ovata*, Tenison-Woods, op. cit., for 1875, p. 17, 1876, *non* Hutton.

Shell pyriformly oval, solid, smooth, shining. Whorls three and a-half, suture thinly covered ; spire obtuse of two and a-half, rapidly increasing, slightly convex whorls ; the apical-half whorl globose, its tip immersed. Last whorl very large, interruptedly moderately convex (being slightly less convex medially); surface marked with slightly sinuous growth-lines (passing into somewhat wrinkled threads at the suture and at the umbilical margin) and interstitial fine striæ, and by inconspicuous revolving threads and towards the suture by fine striæ. Aperture semi-lunar, oblique; outer lip thin, slightly sinuated (projecting slightly forward in an alignment with the inner edge of the callus; columellar callus narrowly and flatly spreading, filling the narrow umbilicus except a conspicuous groove leading into it from the front.

Dimensions.—Length, 19; breadth, 14; diameter of aperture, 12·5; radius of aperture, 7·5.

Locality.—Eocene; "Crassatella-beds" at Table Cape, Tasmania !

Remarks.—In 1876 Tenison-Woods recorded a not uncommon *Natica* in the Table Cape beds as *N. ovata*, Hutton. I fail to find any such species among the various collections examined from that locality, and conclude that the subsequently described species, *N. vix-umbilicata*, was mistaken for it. Johnston ("Geol. Tasmania," 1888), however, retains both names.

N. vix-umbilicata is very much like *N. ovata*, Hutton. Compared with specimens of the latter from the Pareora River (Hutton's figure of this species, "Pliocene Moll. of New Zealand," in Macleay Memorial Volume, 1893, tab. 7, fig. 40, very imperfectly represents the shell obtained from the lower horizon), the present species is of much smaller size, slightly narrower, of fewer whorls, apex immersed, callosity not so extensive, and by the presence of an umbilical chink.

Among recent species, it has analogy with *N. conica*, but has not the elongate spire of that shell; but more so with *N. mammilla*, from which it differs by regularly convex body-whorl, proportionately wider.

5. Natica balteatella, *spec. nov.* Pl. vi., fig. 7.

Shell solid, narrow-oval-conic; whorls five, moderately convex, suture concealed by a thin adpressed extension from anterior whorl. Surface smooth, shining; ornamented by growth-lines (which are abruptly bent and develop into wrinkles on the antesutural band), coincident striæ and distant spiral striæ; a broadish band in front of the suture is conspicuously wavy-striated spirally, the spiral striæ being interrupted by the sharply-angled growth-folds, and by coincident striæ.

Aperture oval, outer lip acute; columella emitting a funicular ridge into the umbilicus, posterior callosity moderate.

Dimensions.—Length, 18·5; width, 7·5; diameter and radius of aperture, 8·5, 6·5; width of umbilicus, 2.

Localities.—MIOCENE, Hallett's Cove (very rare). Older Pliocene, Dry Creek-bore (very common).

This species has much resemblance to a young *N. conica*, but by its umbilicus is more akin to *N. subvarians ;* the sculptured band in front of the umbilicus is a prominent distinctive feature.

6. Natica subvarians, *spec. nov.* Pl. vi., figs. 8, 10.

I apply this name to a shell, related to *N. varians*, but not connected with it by intermediate grades, from which it is distinguished by it elongate-oval outline and produced spire. From the recent *N. conica*, it is separable by its regularly-convex whorls, more open umbilicus with distinct funiculus. Fig. 6 represents a short spired variety.

Dimensions.—Length, 24 : width, 17 : length of aperture, 13.

Localities. — EOCENE, Cheltenham (very rare)!.; MIOCENE, Jemmy's Point and Cunningham, Gippsland!.; Hallett's Cove. and Aldinga Bay !.

7. Natica varians, *spec. nov.* Pl. vi., figs. 2, 9.

Shell solid, globulose-oval to pyriform-conic ; spire very short, obtuse ; whorls five, of rapid increase, suture concealed : last whorl very large and ventricose, usually, at least in the Muddy Creek specimens, slightly depressed on the back. Surface smooth and shining, ornamented with growth-lines and close reticulate striæ, the spiral striæ somewhat wavy. Umbilicus of moderate size, funiculus narrow, terminating on the columella in a moderate-sized callosity : columella thick, largely and thickly spreading posteriorly and over the hinder part of the umbilicus : the posterior callosity separated from the funicular callosity by a notch.

Dimensions.—(a) fig. 3. Length, 40 ; width, 32 : length of aperrure, 31·5 ; width, 17. *(b)* fig. 4. Length, 41·5 ; width, 36 ; length of aperture, 36 ; width, 18·5.

Actual dimensions fail to convey the variability in shape presented by this species : but I have figured two somewhat extreme forms.

Localities.—Miocene (a common fossil) ; Jemmy's Point and Cunningham, Gippsland !.; Muddy Creek !.

Remarks.—*N. varians* has resemblance to *N. Powisiana, N. effusa, N. intermereta, N. unimaculata*, and some other *Mammæ* of the North Pacific shores ; the variation in shape and length of spire would permit of attachment to several of the above, but viewed in its composite character it appears to be distinguished by the fine reticulated ornament.

8. Natica Wintlei, *Tenison-Woods.*

Proc. Roy. Soc., Tasmania for 1875, t. 1, fig. 3, 1876.

Shell shining, stout, ventricosely subglobulose, umbilicated.

Whorls five and a-half to six, suture linear : spire obtuse, elongate ; whorls rounded, slightly flatted posteriorly : one and a-half apical whorls depressed. Surface with fine growth-lines and coincident striae ; faintly and distantly spirally-lined, especially on the base ; spirally striate on the depressed area in front of the suture. Aperture lunately-oval slightly oblique : outer lip acute not sinuate, basal lip incrassated. Umbilicus with a funicular rib : columella, posterior to the funicle, slightly dilated and confluent with the funicular termination, otherwise the umbilicus is narrow.

Dimensions of a moderately large specimen :—Length, 25·5 : breadth, 21 ; vertical height of aperture, 18 : radius of aperture, 10 ; diameter of umbilicus, 3. The proportion of the height to the breadth varies between 100 to 80 and 100 to 82 ; but a few examples from Table Cape have the relative values 100 and 84.

Localities.—Eocene : Crassatella-beds, Table Cape (common) ! : basal beds of the Bird Rock-bluff, Spring Creek (abundant and large) !.

9. Natica Mooraboolensis, *spec. nov.* Pl. vi., fig. 5.

Shell globose, solid, smooth ; whorls five ; apex small, pointed : penultimate whorl flatly convex in posterior two-thirds, somewhat precipitously arching to the anterior suture, which is concealed : last whorl very ventricose, slantingly flattened behind. Aperture semilunate : columella stout, largely expanded behind the umbilicus, which is of moderate width, apparently simple and shallow.

Dimensions.—Length, 28; breadth, 27·5; width of umbilicus, 5.

Locality. Eocene subcrystalline limestone on the Moorabool-river, near Geelong (one example by Mr. G. Sweet).

This species is related to *N. substolida*, but has a more elevated spire, with the whorls flatly sloping behind. Among living shells it most nearly resembles *N. plumbea*, but is more globose, whorls flattened behind, shorter spire, and larger umbilicus.

10. Natica substolida, *spec. nov.* Pl. vi., fig. 3.

Shell solid, oval-globulose, subsphærical; spire conoid, very short, apex obtuse : whorls four narrow, thinly overlapping at the suture : body-whorl very large and convex. Surface smooth and shining, faintly lined and striated spirally, more conspicuously so on the base, crossed by slightly sigmoid incised lines and obscure threads, which at the suture give rise to a narrow wrinkled-band.

Aperture oblique, regularly semilunate : outer lip acute, slightly insinuated posteriorly ; umbilicus simple : columella thick, largely expanding above the umbilicus to form a thick depressed callosity.

W

Dimensions.—Length, 23 ; breadth, 21 ; diameter of aperture, 19 ; radius of aperture, 12.

Localities.—EOCENE : A common shell at Muddy Creek and River Murray Cliffs! ; Cheltenham! ; Camperdown!. MIOCENE : Kalima, Gippsland Lakes ! (rare and small).

Remarks.—This species is closely allied to *N. repanda*, Desh., but is distinguished by more convex body-whorl, more oblique aperture, and more obtuse and smaller spire. *N. substolida* connects the section *Naticina*, through *N. subinfundibulum*, with *Sigaretopsis.*

The specimens from the Murray-river Cliffs are smaller and have the umbilicus more concealed by the columella-callosity than those from Muddy Creek.

11. Natica arata, *spec. nov.* Pl. x., fig. 8.

Shell solid, globulose, subsphærical ; spire excessively short, apex obtuse ; whorls four and a-half, separated by a linear impressed suture ; apical whorls two and a-half, smooth, flatly convex ; the succeeding half turn with about twelve equi-distant transverse sulcations producing a crenulate margin at the posterior suture ; the surface of the remainder of the whorls linear-sulcate spirally ; at first the interspaces are slightly elevated, about equal in width to the sulci and slightly granulated by radial threads ; finally, on the body-whorl the interspaces are flat and broad, about 1 mm. wide on the medial part, and ·5 or less at the base and near the suture ; obscurely lined transversely and inconspicuously wrinkled at the suture. Aperture regularly semilunate ; outer lip bevelled to a thin edge ; columella straight, nearly vertical, rather thick, callously thinly expanding beyond the umbilicus to join with the outer lip ; umbilicus wide, deep, and simple.

Dimensions.—Length and width, 18 ; diameter and radius of aperture, 15 and 9·5 ; width of umbilicus, 3.

Locality.—Eocene calciferous sandstone, River Murray Cliffs (rare) ! ; Muddy Creek (one ex. !);

12. Natica limata, *spec. nov.* Pl. x., fig. 4.

Shell thin, fragile, globose ; spire short, broadly conic, obtuse ; apical whorls two and a-half, shining, smooth, depressedly convex ; the other whorls (two and a-half) regularly and moderately convex, of moderate increase, separated by a narrow, deeply-impressed suture.

Ornament of crowded, raised, wavy threads, sometimes linear at other times several times broader and flat, interrupted by transverse incised lines and striæ ; wrinkled at the suture, but only prominently so on the early spire-whorls.

Aperture regularly semilunate, nearly erect; outer lip thin; columella-margin thin, thinly and freely everted posteriorly, joined by a callous film to the outer lip. Umbilicus wide, simple, the ornament of the body-whorl entering the cavity.

Dimensions.—Length, 18·5; width, 18; diameter and radius of aperture, 14 and 9: width of umbilicus, 3.

Localities.—Eocene: Muddy Creek (rare)!: River Murray Cliffs (very rare)!; Mornington!; and Spring Creek (very rare)!.

13. Natica polita, *Tenison-Woods.*

Proc. Roy. Soc. Tasm., for 1875, p. 23, t. 1, f. 4 (1846) (fig. not good).

Shell shining, moderately stout, ventricosely sub-globulose, umbilicated. Whorls four and a-half, separated usually by a profundly canaliculate suture. Aperture semilunate, slightly oblique: outer lip obtuse, not at all arched. Surface smooth or transversely finely striate, and faintly spirally lined.

Dimensions.—The shell varies in the height of the spire, and much in size; an averaged sized specimen measures, long. 8·75, lat. 7·5 to 7·25, umbilicus 1. Some extremely low-spired forms, with which is invariably associated an ill-defined channelled suture and wider umbilicus (about 2 mm.), give the following measures: ---long. 8·5, lat. 9·5 (River Murray): 13·5 by 13·5 (Table Cape); this variety which I will name *inflata* approaches in shape to *N. Hamiltonensis.*

Localities.—*Forma typica*, EOCENE: Table Cape!; Muddy Creek, also as derived in the upper beds (Miocene)!; Mornington!; Cheltenham!: Gellibrand River!; Belmont!;· River Murray Cliffs!; Shelford!. MIOCENE: Jemmy's Point (a single dwarf ex.!), *Forma inflata:* Table Cape!; River Murray Cliffs!; Fyansford!; Bird-rock Bluff (chiefly intermediate between *forma typica* and *var. inflata*)!; Bellarine Peninsula!.

Remarks.—Tenison-Woods (Proc. Roy. Soc. Tasm. for 1877, p. 32, 1878) records *N. polita*, also, as a recent shell on the Tasmanian Coast. Johnston (id. for 1884, p. 221, 1885) adduces the following distinctions for the separation of the living analogue under the name of *N. Beddomei:*—

" In the living form the spire is more depressed, and the whorls increase more rapidly in size. In the fossil form the nucleus is invariably smaller than in the living representative, and the number of whorls in mature specimens is four and a-half. In the living mature form the number of whorls is invariably three and a-half. The aperture in both does not present any marked difference, if we except the fact that, in the fossil state, the inner margin is almost vertical. In the living form, the same feature is more decidedly angled relative to a central line drawn through the nucleus. If anything the fossil shell is larger and more solid, although it must be stated, that, if an immature fossil shell be selected for comparison with only the same number of whorls developed as in the mature living form, the latter seems to be the broader of the two."

14. Natica perspectiva, *spec. nov.* Pl. x., fig. 7.

Shell thin, globular, spire short, conic, somewhat obtuse ; whorls four and a-half, narrow, ventricose, slightly depressed in front of the suture ; suture linear impressed. Surface smooth, shining, ornamented with striæ of growth ; obsoletely wavy-striated spirally, more conspicuous on base of body-whorl. Aperture regularly semilunate, erect ; outer lip thin : columella-margin thin, thinly and freely everted posteriorly, joined by a callous film to the outer lip. Umbilicus broad, profund, simple, defined by an obtuse keel confluent with the basal angle of the aperture which is there thickened ; the columella-wall of the umbilicus is somewhat concave, vertically and transversely lined.

Dimensions.—Length, 17 : width, 16·5 : base and radius of aperture, 12·5 and 8 ; width on umbilicus, 4.

Localities.—EOCENE : Muddy Creek (common)! : Mornington! : Gellibrand River! : Camperdown! ; Cheltenham!. MIOCENE : Gippsland (one ex. !).

Affinities.—*N. perspectiva* is related to *N. limata*, but it has more convex whorls, body-whorl much larger, larger umbilicus defined by a keel : from *N. polita* it is separable by its globose form, narrow suture, and wide umbilicus. Among exotic species it has a near ally in *N. semilunata*, Lea, of the Alabama-Eocene from which it differs chiefly in its impressed suture.

15. Natica Aldingensis, *spec. nov.* Pl. x., fig. 5.

Shell moderately solid, somewhat intermediate in shape between *N. limata* and *N. perspectiva*, but with a shorter spire, and though the suture is open yet it is not distinctly channelled as in those species ; the umbilicus is like that of *limata*, but is much narrower.

Surface ornamented with striæ and lines of growth, the latter raised into slight wrinkles at the suture, and obsolete spiral lines and striæ.

From *N. semilunata* it is distinguished by its more ventricose spire-whorls and small umbilicus.

Dimensions.—Length, 19 : width, 18 : diameter and radius of aperture 19 and 9·5 : width of umbilicus, 2·5.

Localities.—EOCENE : Aldinga Cliffs (common) : and Adelaide-bore.

16. Natica subinfundibulum, *spec. nov.* Pl. x., fig. 11; pl. vi., fig. 6.

Shell usually rather thin, depressed, auriform: spire very short, obtuse: whorls three, suture concealed. Surface with crowded, curved, transverse lines, which coalesce at the suture in slight folds. Spiral lines distant and faint, two or three less indistinct at the suture. Aperture obliquely lunate, outer and basal margins acute; columella nearly vertical, the posterior-half somewhat thickened, slightly reflected, and joined to the outer lip. Umbilicus very large and perspective; columella-wall of the umbilicus slightly concave, or with an ill-defined medial ridge, distantly spirally-lined and axially closely striate. The edge of the umbilical depression either slopes gradually inwards or is abruptly defined.

Dimensions.—Length and width, 13: height, 8: basal length of aperture, 12: width of umbilicus, 4·5.

Localities.—EOCENE: Muddy Creek!; Mornington! Gellibrand River!: Fyansford!; Cheltenham!: Murray-river Cliffs!. MIOCENE: Muddy Creek!; Gippsland!.

Affinities.—This third species of the section *Sigaretopsis*, established by Cossmann (Soc. Roy. Malac. Belgique, vol. XXIII., p. 168, 1888) differs, by comparison of actual specimens, from *N. infundibulum*, Wat., by narrower and more convex body-whorl, and by more obtuse spire. Deshayes' figures of *N. Woodi* represent a more globulose shell, with a much-less open umbilicus.

I would place in this section *Natica umbilicata*, Quoy and Gaimard, recent on the coast of Southern Australia, which is referred to *Mamilla* by Tryon. Our fossil species is more compressed and vaulted, and has a much wider umbilicus.

Varieties.—VAR. CRASSA is distinguished simply by its thick test and usually larger size, attaining to 20 mm. in length and width. It occurs at Muddy Creek in the lower and upper beds; sometimes as a derived fossil, though rarely *in situ*, in the latter; also at Cheltenham, where the largest specimens occur. VAR. RHYSA, in which the spiral ornament consists of close-set wavy threads. A single example from the River Murray Cliffs. But some specimens of *var. crassa* from Muddy Creek exhibit this ornamentation in a less conspicuous way, graduating to the typical form in which it is obsolete.

GENUS AMPULLINA.

SECTION EUSPIRA.

Ampullina effusa, *spec. nov.* Pl. x., figs. 2, 2a.

Shell acuminately globose, elongate: test thin and fragile; whorls eight and a-half, convex, slightly flattened in front of suture: suture simple, linearly impressed: spire elongate, regularly conical, whorls of slow increase, apex erect with the tip immersed. Surface ornamented by crowded spiral striæ, broken up into narrow ('5-·75 mm.) transverse bands by slightly curved incised lines.

Last whorl globulose, large, a little higher than the length of the spire. Aperture somewhat oblique, semilunate ; outer and basal margins effusively dilated ; outer lip slightly ascending, thin ; columella thinly everted ; umbilicus simple, rather narrow, partly concealed by the everted columella border.

Dimensions.—Length, 35 ; width, 24 ; height of aperture, 21 ; width of aperture, 13 , width of umbilicus, 2 *(cir.).*

Locality.—Eocene : Glauconitic clayey sands, Adelaide-bore (many examples).

Remarks.—This interesting species is certainly congeneric with *Natica acuminata*, Lamk., and *N. Leresquei*, D'Orb., transferred by Cossmann to the section *Euspira* of the genus *Ampullina*. It agrees with them in the elevated and canaliculate spire, but is readily distinguished by its regular spire (not subulate), effusively dilated aperture, and elegant sculpture ; from *A. acuminata*, it is further removed by being umbilicated, but resembles *A. Leresquei* in its simple umbilicus.

GENUS SIGARETUS.

Sigaretus microstira, *spec. nov.* Pl. vii., fig. 10.

Shell depressed, narrow oblong-oval ; spire short, not at all prominent ; suture concealed ; columella slightly thickened and narrowly reflected, forming an open umbilical fissure. The ornamentation consists of conspicuous undulations and coincident striæ, and of very slender and distant spiral threads and coincident striæ ; the spiral ornament is hardly visible by the unaided eye, and is confined to the median and posterior portions of the body-whorl ; the spiral threads are closer together (the interspaces only two or three times wider) and are more prominent posteriorly, which are there conspicuously reticulated by the transverse striæ.

Dimensions.—Length, 18 ; breadth, 13 ; height, 7.

Locality.—Eocene : Bird-rock Bluff (two examples).

Affinities.—This new species has a resemblance in outline and elevation of spire to *S. Cuvierianus*, Recluz. The umbilical fissure is open, not covered by a reflection of the columella, as is usual among living congeners, in this particular *S. microstira* is related to *C. clathratus* and some other species in the Eocene of Europe, from all of which it differs by its depressed and elongate shape.

Heligmope, *gen. nov.*

Etymology—*heligmos*, a sinuosity ; *ope*, an aperture.

Shell oval-globulose, thin, not pearly, imperforate : aperture large, oblique ; columella thin, truncated anteriorly ; basal margin of aperture *insinuated*.

The genus may be described as an imperforate *Eunaticina*, or a *Sigaretus*, with a sinuated front margin, and stands in relation to it as *Protoma* does to *Turritella*. The non-perlaceous test removes it from the neighbourhood of *Stomatella*.

Heligmope Dennanti, *spec. nov.* Pl. vii., figs. 5-5a.

Shell rather thin, oval, convex [or somewhat depressed-orbicular] ; spire moderately prominent [or depressed]. Whorls four and a-half, suture more or less concealed by the adpressed reflection from the anterior whorl. Ornament of slightly elevated, rounded, spiral ribs, about ten on body-whorl [sometimes the spiral ribs are almost obsolete], narrower than the flatly concave furrows, crossed by close-set lamelliform striae, which become wider apart and more distinctly lamellar with the decreasing revolution of the spire.

Aperture oblique, oblong-oval [or semicircular] ; outer lip acute, crenulated by the spiral ribs ; columella cylindric, thinly reflected posteriorly and adherent over the umbilical area ; the lamellae of the back intersect the sinus-band.

The words included in parentheses in the foregoing diagnosis refer to the majority of the specimens obtained from Hallett's Cove, and thus markedly differ from the figured specimens which I select as types and with which all the Muddy Creek specimens agree ; though from the former locality I have a fairly typical specimen, otherwise I should have been disposed to regard the depressed form as a distinct species.

Dimensions.—Length, 32 ; width, 27·5 ; height and width of aperture, 25 and 16.

Localities.—Miocene : Muddy Creek, Victoria, and Hallett's Cove, St. Vincent Gulf

This species was first brought to my notice by Mr. J. Dennant, who kindly forwarded me the figured examples, after whom it is named.

FAMILY HIPPONYCIDÆ.

GENUS HIPPONYX.

Hipponyx antiquatus, *Lin.*

H. foliacea, Quoy and Gaimard, Voy. Astrolabe, vol. III., p. 439, pl. 72, figs. 41-45.

A *Capulus*-like shell with concentric laminations and radial threads.

Habitat.—EOCENE and MIOCENE : Muddy Creek ! RECENT : Australia, Polynesia, &c.

Hipponyx australis, *Lamarck*.

H. australis, Quoy and Gaimard, op. cit., p. 434, pl. 72, figs. 25-34.

Differs from *H. antiquatus* by its broadish flat radiating ribs ribs separated by narrow interstices.

Habitat.—Miocene: Hallett's Cove, St. Vincent Gulf!; and Muddy Creek! Newer Pliocene: Limestone Creek, Dartmoor *(J. Dennant.')*. Recent: Australia, New Zealand, &c.

FAMILY CALYPTRÆIDÆ.

Genus Crepidula.

Synopsis of Species.

Apex terminal.	1. *unguiformis.*
Apex submarginal.	2. *dubitabilis.*
Apex posterior, but distant, hooked.	3. *Hainsworthi.*

1. Crepidula unguiformis, *Lamarck*.

Id., Reeve, Conch. Icon., fig. 1.

Forma typica.—Upper surface flat or concave.

Habitat.—Miocene, Gippsland !. Fossil specimens have been compared with living examples from east coast of N. America and from Southern Australia. [Also Pliocene, Wanganui, &c., New Zealand. Recent, almost cosmopolitan.]

Forma convexa.—(Syn. *C. immersa*, Angas). Upper surface convex.

Habitat.—Eocene: Muddy Creek !; Cheltenham !; Table Cape !. Recent: South Australia, &c.

Forma inflata.—(Syn. *C. monoxyla*, Lesson). Upper surface very convex; resembles *C. fornicata* without radial ridges.

Habitat. -Eocene: Muddy Creek !. Miocene: Muddy Creek (specimens faintly ridged) !. Newer Pliocene: Limestone Creek *(J. Dennant.')*. Recent: New Zealand, and also in Pliocene strata at Wanganui, Petane, &c.

2. Crepidula dubitabilis, *spec. nov.* Pl. ix., fig. 5.

Shell like *C. monoxyla*, but the small spiral apex is narrowly separated from the margin. It, however, varies from convexedly depressed to moderately inflated.

Dimensions of a medium specimen :—Length, 25 ; width, 16 ; height, 8.

Localities. — Eocene: River Murray Cliffs !; Mornington !. Miocene: Gippsland lakes !

3. Crepidula Hainsworthi, *Johnston*.

Ref.—Proc. Roy. Soc. Tasmania for 1884, p. 333, figs. *a-c*, 1885 ; *id.*, Geol. Tasmania, t. 32, f. 13, 1888.

Basal outline oval, narrowly and abruptly arched laterally,

and gently rounded longitudinally : surface with fine growth-lines ; beak hooked, posterior, projecting beyond the posterior margin.

Dimensions.—Length, 14 ; breadth, 8 ; height, 5·5 mm.

Locality.—EOCENE : Table Cape *(J. M. Johnston).*

GENUS CALYTRAEA.

SYNOPSIS OF SPECIES.

Axis imperforate (CALYPTRAEA, *s.s.*).
Shell depressed, apex subcentral.
  Concentrically corrugated, interruptedly convex.
                            1.   *corrugata.*
  Concentrically lamellose-striate, regularly convex.
                            2.   *placuna.*
Spire elevated, apex lateral or subcentral.
  Whorls ventricose, posteriorly flattened. 3. *subtabulata.*
  Whorls regularly convex.
    Spire narrow-conic ; finely lamellate-striate concentrically; spirally-lined. 4. *undulata.*
    Spire broad-conic : concentrically lamellose.
                            5.   *crassa.*
Axis umbilicate (CALYPTROPSIS) depressedly convex, apex very excentric.
  Body-whorl ventricose : base subcircular.
    Concentrically lined, radially lined and striated.
                         6. *arachnoideus.*
  Body-whorl flatly sloping posteriorly.
    Base subcircular, slender radial and concentric threads.
                         7. *turbinata.*
  Base oval, radially costated, finely lamellose, striated concentrically, body-whorl much depressed. 8. *umbilicata.*

1. Calyptraea corrugata, *spec. nov.* Pl. vii., fig. 9.

Shell depressed, orbicular in basal outline, sub-pellucid ; body-whorl more or less ventricose around the suture, surface irregularly concentrically ridged : edge of septum slightly arched.

Similar to *C. pellucida*, Reeve, with specimens of which I have compared it : but differs by interruptedly-convex whorls and strong growth-folds.

Dimensions.—Basal diameters, 12 and 11 : height, 3·5.

Localities.—Miocene : Muddy Creek and at Nor'-west Bend, River Murray.

2. Calyptraea placuna, *spec. nov.* Pl. vii., fig. 4.

Shell depressed, thin, fragile, orbicular in basal outline : body-whorl regularly convex, anterior surface slenderly lamellate concentrically, becoming posteriorly striate.

Dimensions.—Basal diameters, 15 and 16 : height, 4·25.
Localities.—Eocene : Aldinga Cliffs and Adelaide-bore.

3. Calyptraea subtabulata, *spec. nov.* Pl. vii., fig. 1.

Syn.—*Trochita calyptraeformis*, R. M. Johnston, Proc. Roy. Soc.,
Tasmania for 1876, p. 86 (1877) : id., "Geol. Tasm.," t. 29, f. 14.

Shell moderately stout, orbicular in basal outline, spire elevated,
subcentral ; apex minute, slightly exsert ; body-whorl conspicuously flattened in front of suture, surface with subimbricating
growth-folds and spiral coarse striæ : septum with a nearly
straight edge.

The shell varies much in height, and the higher the spire the
more tabulated are the whorls, the figured specimen represents
the most commonly-occurring form.

Dimensions.— Basal diameters, 29·5 and 26·5 ; height, 12.

Locality.—Eocene: Table Cape, Tasmania, *R. M. Johnston*, &c. !

This abundant fossil at Table Cape was referred by Johnston
to the living Australian shell, *Trochus calyptraeformis*, Lamarck
(=*Calyptraea tomentosa*, Quoy and G.), to which, however, it has
only a distant resemblance.

Pileopsis naricelloides, R. M. Johnston, Poc. Roy. Soc.,
Tasmania, for 1879, p. 39 (1880), is probably a *Calyptraea*, and
possibly a very young state of *C. subtabulata*. The original
diagnosis reads as follows :—Shell minute, depressed, subrotund ;
nucleus scarcely lax, exserted, of about one and a half smooth
turns, submarginal ; disk with rough uneven surface, concentrically irregularly striate : aperture ovate, closed at posterior
margin by a *spiral concave* shelf, terminating on either side by a
downward reflexed curve in the muscular impressions, which are
well-defined. Dia. mag., 3·5 : min., 3 : alt., 1. Table Cape
(one specimen).

4. Calyptraea undulata, *spec. nov.* Pl. vii., fig. 3.

Shell thin, orbicular in basal outline : spire elevated, subcentral, of rather rapidly increasing, steep-sloping whorls ; apex
minute, oblique, circinately-coiled ; body-whorl regularly convex ;
surface concentrically ridged and coincidently striated, faintly
spirally-lined ; septum with a nearly straight edge.

Dimensions.—Major and minor diameters, 16·5 and 15·5 ;
height, 8.

Localities.—Eocene : Muddy Creek ; River Murray Cliffs.

Differs from *C. subtabulata* by regular convex whorls and more
excentric spire.

5. Calyptraea crassa, *spec. nov.* Pl. vii., figs. 2, 7.

Shell rather stout, orbicular in basal outline ; spire elevated,
subcentral of rapidly increasing, moderately convex whorls ;

apex small, oblique, circinately coiled ; body-whorl regularly flatly convex, concentrically lamellose-ridged ; septum with a concave edge.

Dimensions.—Diameters, 27 and 25 : height, 11.

Localities.—Miocene : Gippsland Lakes (common)! ; Hallett's Cove !.

Differs from *C. undulata*, by its less excentric apex and less ventricose whorls.

SUBGENUS CALYPTROPIS, *Tate.*

Ref.—Proc. Roy. Soc., N.S. Wales, vol. XXVII., p. 181, 1893. "Shell like *Calptraea*, but umbilicated, and with a columella-insinuosity at the umbilical border.

6. Calyptropsis arachnoideus, *spec. nov.* Pl. vii., fig. 9.

Shell thin, orbicular in basal outline ; spire depressed, apex submarginal, of rapidly increasing, ventricose whorls ; surface ornamented with acute raised concentric threads and distant similar spiral threads : the interspaces with close, raised striæ ; septum slightly ecurved medially, slightly concave, faintly radiately ridged.

Dimensions.—Diameters, 12·5 and 10·5 : height, 4·25.

Localities.—Eocene : Aldinga Cliffs and Adelaide-bore (very rare.

7. Calyptropsis turbinata, *Ten.-Woods.*

Trochita turbinata, Ten.-Woods, Proc. Lin. Soc., N.S. Wales, vol. III., p. 238, pl. 21, fig. 1, 1879.

Shell thin, suborbicular in basal outline, turbinately depressed ; whorls two and a-half, rapidly increasing, somewhat flattened posteriorly, apex exsert; surface slightly corrugated concentrically, and coincidently finely lined ; spirally distantly lined, faintly ridged on posterior area of body-whorl : septum deeply sunk, radiately sulcate ; umbilicus narrow.

Dimensions.—Diameters, 11 and 10 ; height, 4·5.

Localities.—Eocene : Muddy Creek *(Tenison-Woods.')* : Bird-rock Bluff, near Geelong !.

8. Calyptropsis umbilicata, *Johnston.*

Crepidula umbilicata, R. M. Johnston, Proc. Roy. Soc. Tasmania for 1884, p. 232 (two figs.), 1885 : id., "Geol. Tasmania, t. 32, fig. 10, 1888.

Shell rather thin, oval in basal outline ; body-whorl depressed, flatly convex, more rapidly sloping from the periphery to the margins ; apex posterior, oblique, submarginal, slightly elevated ; whorls two and a-half of very rapid increase : surface somewhat rugose with a few distant spiral ridges crossed by lamellæ of growth, and coincident fine striæ. Septum flat or slightly concave, its margin nearly straight; umbilicus moderately wide profund.

Dimensions.—Diameters, 17 and 13 ; height, 5.

Locality.—Table Cape *(R. M. Johnston !).*

Genus CAPULUS.

Syn.—Pileopsis, Lamk.

SPECIES EXCLUDED.

Pileopsis naricelloides, Johnston, is transferred to *Calyptraea.*

1. Capulus circinatus, *spec. nov.* Pl. vii., fig. 8.

Shell cornucopia-shaped with a spiral recurved slightly excentric apex, base roundly oval, sides slightly compressed; whorls two and a-half, the anterior one detached ; surface with fine radial threads crossed by slender folds and fine threads which are arched medially.

Dimensions.—Diameters, 2·5 and 2 : height, 3·25.

Locality.—Eocene : Adelaide-bore (one ex.).

2. Capulus Danieli, *Crosse.*

Syn.—C subrufus, Sowerby, *non* Lamk.

The fossils, which I refer to the living species of this name, have been compared with specimens of a species usually known in Southern Australian waters as *Capulus subrufus,* Sowb., the larger forms of which have received Crosse's name, as the result of comparison of authenticated examples from New Caledonia.

Tyron places the species in the genus *Hipponyx,* but as no shelly base is formed, I retain it in *Capulus.*

The shell has somewhat compressed sides, an irregular orbicular base, but it is variable in these particulars, as largely dependent on the outline of the surface of attachment ; the apex is posterior usually turned to the left, and either prolonged or subspirally hooked.

The fossil specimens exhibit equal variation of shape and form of apex, as do the recent ones, but seem to be devoid of fine radial ridges, and thus present the usual aspect of beach-shells.

Localities.—Eocene : Muddy Creek !. Miocene : Aldinga Cliffs and Muddy Creek !.

FAMILY TURRITELLIDÆ.

Genus TURRITELLA.

From the great variability in form and sculpture of the majority of our fossil-species of this genus, one is tempted to conclude that no satisfactory position can be taken up anywhere between the extremes regarding the whole genus as an enormous protean species, or describing nearly every colony as a separate species. Here characters can be seen varying in all directions, and in almost all degrees, though some variations seem to be fixed, whilst others remain indefinite. This is very perplexing in the definition of species, though to the student of evolution this difficulty will be full of interest.

Specimens presenting a sinus in the outer lip are too rare (and so far only observed in two species) to use this feature in the arrangement of the species, but the form of curvature, which the incremental lines present, may prove of importance : the exigencies of publication have, however, prevented me testing fully the classificatory value of this character.

The internal septation, which is exhibited by two of our species (*T. septifraga*, in which it is invariable and frequent, and *T. tristira*, observed in one instance), is a feature hitherto unrecorded in the genus.

SYNOPSIS OF SPECIES.

Whorls smooth, or not distinctly lirate, subimbricating.
 Shell very elongate, posterior whorls medially carinate.
             1. *septifraga.*
 Shell under 15 mm., anterior whorls ridged posteriorly.
             2. *pagodula.*
Whorls carinate and lirate.
 Keels granulose.
  Keels three, median granulose.   3. *Aldingae.*
  Keels three, anterior and median granulose.
             4. *Warburtoni.*
  Keels three, middle one granulose. 5. *Sturtii.*
  Keels four to five, all granulose. 6. *gemmulata.*
 Keels not granulose.
  Keels three, equal.   7. *tristira.*
  Keel one, very prominent.   8. *conspicabilis.*
  Keels two, whorls imbricate.   9. *acricula.*
Whorls lirate.
 Lirae numerous, squamose, whorls medially concave.
           10. *Murrayana.*
 Lirae under 20, more or less unequal, whorls flat or imbricate : shell slender.   9. *acricula.*
 Lirae five or less, whorls flat or slightly convex.
           11. *platyspira.*

SPECIES EXCLUDED.

Turritella transenna, Tenison-Woods, Proc. Lin. Soc., vol. III., p. 234, an Eocene-fossil at Muddy Creek, is transferred to *Mathilda.*

1. Turritella septifraga, *spec. nov.* Pl. viii., fig. 5.

Shell narrowly lanceolate-turreted ; whorls 18, apex unknown anterior whorls concave, sloping to the sharp angulation at (and somewhat imbricating over) the anterior suture ; posterior whorls flat or very slightly concave, slightly keeled in the anterior-fourth, suture linear.

Surface ornamented with deeply sinuous, crowded, fine striæ of growth ; the anterior keel of the anterior whorls two to three lined, faintly and distantly lined on the concave area.

Aperture subquadrangular, outer lip with a broad, moderately-deep sinus (that is judging from growth-lines).

The interior is septated at every two or three whorls throughout the posterior-half of the length of the shell; and the facility with which the shell breaks at these junctions has suggested the specific name.

Dimensions.—Length (incomplete), 100 ; width, 17.

Locality.—Eocene : Bird-rock Bluff, Geelong !.

The absence of conspicuous spiral ornament removes this species from somewhat similar congeners, such as *T. Cumingii*, Reeve, *T. imbricataria*, Lk., &c.

2. Turritella pagodula, *spec. nov.* Pl. viii., fig. 10.

Shell small, acuminately turreted ; whorls thirteen (incl. embryo), with a prominent roundly-angled ridge over the anterior suture, with or without a less conspicuous ridge at the posterior suture; apical whorls two, very small, inflated; posterior spire-whorls keeled over the suture. Surface smooth, shining, closely insinuate-striate transversely and faintly spirally-lined in the concave area between the anterior and posterior ridges. Periphery of body-whorl subtended by a subordinate keel ; base with about ten concentric threads crossed by radial striæ. Aperture subquadrangular ; outer lip with a semicircular insinuation above the anterior keel.

Dimensions.—Length, 12·5 ; width, 4·25.

Locality.—Miocene : Gippsland Lakes (not uncommon !).

This species has some affinity with the recent *T. exoleta*, Linn., but its small size and obsolete posterior ridge distinguish it; also with *T. granulifera*, Tenison-Woods, which is, however, conspicuously different by its granulated keels ; and more so with *T. terebellata*, Tate, *m.s.*, Newer Pliocene, Limestone Creek, W. Victoria, which has the anterior keel nodulose.

3. Turritella Aldingæ, *Tate.* Pl. viii., fig. 1.

Reference.—Trans. Roy. Soc. S. Aust., vol. V., p. 45, 1882.

Shell acutely pryamidal, a little more than three times as long as broad, whorls about twenty in a length of 33 mm., subquadrate or flattish with three prominent ribs, moderately impressed suture, the medial ones usually granulose. Base flattened, ornamented with many unequal-sized spiral threads, which are crossed by very fine radial striæ. Aperture subquadrate, margins united by a somewhat thick callus, which extends over much of the base; columella arched, regularly curving to the rounded basal lip; outer lip somewhat flatly compressed, deeply and broadly sinuated.

The ornament on the whorls varies much in different specimens, as well as in different parts of the same shell. The medium prominent rib is generally granulose; the posterior rib is bisulcated, or not infrequently replaced by two or three strong threads; the interspaces between the ribs and adjacent to the sutures are ornamented with a few spiral threads crossed by curved lines of growth. On the anterior whorls of large examples there are about eight unequalled-sized spiral ribs—the posterior rib on the earlier whorls has developed into three prominent ribs, and one or more of the intermediate threads have become conspicuous, whilst the granulations of the medium rib have disappeared.

The posterior six whorls or so have occasionally all the ribs granulose, thus resembling *T. Sturtii*; but at this early stage *T. Aldingæ* does not possess intermediate ribs.

Dimensions.—Length, 36 : breadth, 10·5; depth and width of sinus, 3.

Localities.—Eocene: Argillaceous limestone and associated clays at Blanche Point, Aldinga Bay (very abundant), and Adelaide-bore !; also in the "Turritella limestone" about Ardrossan, Yorke Peninsula *(J. G. O. Tepper.')*.

In outline, general shape of whorls, and deep sinus, this fossil species has an analogue in *T. runcinata*, Watson, "Challenger" Gasteropoda, p. 475, t. 30, fig. 3; compared with actual specimens of which, the fossil is conspicuously distinguished by curved columella (not straight in the axis, and effusively dilated at the front), and tricarinate whorls.

4. Turritella Warburtoni, *Ten.-Woods.* Pl. viii., fig. 2.

Shell small, narrowly pyramidal; whorls 15, in a length of 9·5 mm.; apex of two and a-half smooth turns, the tip subglobulose, the next turn narrow and convex; ordinary whorls concave, separated by a narrow deeply impressed suture, roundly elevated at the posterior suture, more angulated and elevated at the anterior suture; posterior to which and near to is a more acute but less stout keel; the two anterior ribs more or less granulose; each of the interspaces between the keels with two or three fine threads of varying size. Growth-lines hardly discernible, slightly

arched.   Base flat, separated from peripheral keel by a deep
groove ; ornamented with about eight spiral ridges.
Aperture quadrate : columella thinly reflected.
Dimensions.—Length, 14 : breadth, 4.
Locality.—Eocene : Table Cape *(Ten.-Woods*, common !).
Has a resemblance to *T. pagodula*, Tate, but is a narrower
shell, and differs in the details of the ornamentation : from
T. granulifera, T.-Wds., to which it bears some resemblance by
its smooth posterior keel and its prominent anterior one.

5. Turritella Sturtii, *Tenison-Woods*.   Pl. viii., fig. 6.

Shell small, acutely pyramidal : whorls fifteen in a length of
12 mm., apex of three small smooth rounded turns : ordinary
whorls constricted at the suture, spirally ribbed ; prominent ribs
three, equidistant, of which the median and anterior ones are
granulose, the posterior one often double, each interspace with
about two fine spiral threads : growth-lines deeply arched.   Base
flattened, angulated at the margin, with seven or eight equal-
sized spiral threads, crossed by numerous very fine striæ.   Aperture subquadrate : outer-lip thin : columella thinly reflected
behind and over the base.
Dimensions.—Length, 22 : breadth, 5·25.
Locality.—Eocene : Abundant in the "Turritella beds," Table
Cape *(Tenison-Woods.')*.

6. Turritella gemmulata, *sper. nov.*   Pl. viii., fig. 11.

Shell minute, narrow lanceolate-turreted ; apex of one and
a-half turns, the tip globulose, the next turn convex, narrow :
whorls nine (excl. embryo), flatly concave, but separated by a
broad, deeply impressed suture ; ornamented by beaded ribs.
decreasing in number from front backwards from five or six to
three, the next but one to the anterior suture usually with the
largest granules : the last three spire-whorls bi- or uni-carinate.
Periphery of body-whorl rounded, base with about five encircling
threads ; aperture rotund, columella thinly reflected.
Dimensions.—Length, 6·5 ; width, 1·75.
Localities.—Eocene : Muddy Creek (not uncommon !) ; Bird-
rock Bluff, Spring Creek (rare !).

7. Turritella tristira, *Tate.*   Pl. viii., fig. 8 : Pl. x., fig. 3.

Ref.—Proc. Roy. Soc., Tasmania, for 1884, p. 227 (1885).
Shell acuminately turreted ; apical angle about 15° ; whorls
seventeen, anterior and medial whorls slightly convex, suture
linear ; apex globulose of one and a half whorls, the tip immersed, the first four or five spire-whorls flatly convex, the next
three or four medially concave.   Surface ornamented with three
conspicuous, acute, spiral ribs, the interspaces with closely and

finely spiral striæ and inconspicuous transverse striæ; the sulci on each side of the central rib are of equal breadth, but the anterior rib is separated from the suture by a distance less than that which intervenes between it and central rib, whilst the posterior rib is separated from its corresponding suture by a distance greater than the breadth of the medial sulcus. Last whorl with four keels, truncately angular at the periphery: base spirally flatly ribbed and interstriated. Aperture quadrate: outer lip imperfect; the striæ of growth deeply roundly arched between the anterior and posterior keels.

Dimensions.—Length, 46; breadth, 12.

Locality.—Eocene: Table Cape *(R. M. Johnston*, one example!): Cheltenham (not uncommon!); Camperdown!; Belmont!; (?) well-sinking, Murray Desert!. Miocene: Gippsland Lakes (very abundant!).

This species is distinct from the few living species, which are conspicuously three-ribbed, by shape, ornament, and the unsymmetrical position of the revolving keels. *T. tricincta*, Hutton. Pliocene and Miocene in New Zealand, has three unequal keels and the whorls more convex.

8. Turritella conspicabilis, *spec. nov.* Pl. viii., fig. 7.

Shell similar to *T. tristira*, but differs in its ornamentation. The spire is acuminately attenuated: the embryonic whorls are succeeded by two or three convex whorls, then follow three or four, which are convex posteriorly, but abruptly declining to the anterior suture: the anterior keel becomes stronger, and on the posterior area threads appear, increasing in number with the revolution of the spire. Anterior whorls have a high rounded rib, situated in the anterior one-third, separated by a wide sulcus from the posterior one-half, which is ornamented by six to ten threads alternately large and small; the anterior-half, including the keel, is spirally striate.

Locality.—Eocene: Spring Creek!. Miocene: Gippsland Lakes!.

Though associated with *T. tristira* at the latter locality, and not with it elsewhere, yet as there are no decided intermediate stages, I have somewhat reluctantly considered it a distinct species. A varietal form (pl. ix., fig. 6), if not a distinct species, occurs abundantly at Spring Creek, which differs by less prominent keel. It makes some approach to that variety of *T. runcinata*, in which the front keel is conspicuously elevated, but the whorls are more quadrate, the keel truncated on the edge; whilst the spiral striæ are fewer and not wavy-interrupted.

9. Turritella acricula, *spec. nov.* Pl. viii., fig. 4; pl. ix., figs. 4, 7, 8.

Shell very acutely lanceolate-turreted; whorls twenty, apex mammillary of two narrow convex turns, early posterior whorls

x

smooth and sharply carinated in the middle, anterior whorls flatly convex to the sharp or blunt angulation at (and somewhat imbricating over) the anterior suture, sometimes the anterior angulation is obsolete. Surface ornamented with spiral threads (about fifteen or more); of these three to five are sharply elevated into slender keels, the medial one of which is usually the most prominent, the interspaces being then finely lirate; rarely are the threads approximately of equal strength. The transverse ornament consists of medially-arched growth-lines, close or rather distant, in the latter case producing the appearance of punctures, sometimes the lines of growth are raised into lamellæ. Periphery of body-whorl acutely angulated, base concentrically ribbed and radially striated. Aperture subquadrangular, slightly oblique, columella nearly straight, thinly reflected and spreading behind; outer lip not seen perfect.

Dimensions.—Length, 38 : breadth, 6·25

Localities.—Eocene : River Murray Cliffs (very abundant!); Sc. Mornington!; Muddy Creek!; Cheltenham!; Corio Bay!; Camperdown!; Gellibrand River!: Spring Creek!; Table Cape. Miocene : Gippsland Lakes!; Aldinga Cliffs (imperfectly determinate!).

This species varies in the form of the whorls and the development of the liræ; a variety occurring at Gellibrand River and Muddy Creek has slightly, though regularly, convex whorls, which are finely lirate (pl. ix., fig. 4); a similar form occurs at Table Cape (pl. iv., fig. 12), but is much stouter, slightly angulated towards the suture, and strongly lirate.

It is separable with difficulty from *T. acuta*, Ten.-Woods, Proc. Roy. Soc. Tasmania, p. 143, 1876, a recent species in S. Australia and Tasmania; they have similar apices, and exhibit the same variation in the extent of imbrication of the whorls; but *T. acricula* is relatively narrower, and has more liræ, whilst in *T. acuta* the liræ never assume the character of keels.

10. Turritella Murrayana, *Tate.* Pl. viii., fig. 3.

Torcula Murrayana, Tate, Proc. Roy. Soc. Tasm., for 1884, p. 227 (1885).

Shell pyramidally turreted, apical angle about 15°. Whorls twelve to fourteen, flattish, medially depressed, and acutely elevated at about the anterior-fourth; suture thread-like or somewhat grooved; apical whorls two, very small, globulose; first spire-whorls rapidly enlarging 1-3 carinate. Surface ornamented by about 24 spiral threads, with or without smaller intermediary ones, crossed by close-set striæ, the latter on the anterior whorls thinly squamose. Last whorl bluntly truncated on the periphery; base with spiral threads and transverse striæ as on the upper part of the whorl.

Aperture quadrately oval, continuous; outer lip with a deepish subtriangular median sinus.

The sectional outline of the whorls varies from flat or slightly concave to somewhat quadrate, and correspondingly in the depth of the suture ; the ante-medial keel is sometimes obsolete, but the medial depression is always present.

Dimensions.—Length, 60 ; breadth, 17 ; height of last whorl, 12.

Localities.—Eocene : River Murray Cliffs (very abundant !); Muddy Creek !: Corio Bay, near Geelong !; Mornington !; Gellibrand River !; Belmont !; Table Cape *(R. M. Johnston.')*. Miocene : Gippsland Lakes (rare !).

T. Murrayana has resemblance to *T. declivis*, Ads. & Reeve, but has not the backward-slanting whorls of that species, which is apparently without a conspicuous sinus in the outer lip. It has also much resemblance to *T. rosea*, Quoy & Gaimard, but in that the spiral ornament of the posterior whorls develop into ribs on the anterior whorls.

The Table Cape specimens have usually flattish or slightly concave whorls with or without the anterior keel, but fall within the limits of variation exhibited by the Murray examples, though they are usually broader in proportion—the apical angle being as much as 18°

11. **Turritella platyspira**, *Tenison-Woods.* Pl. viii., fig. 9.

Ref.—Proc. Lin. Soc. N.S.W., vol. III, p. 234, t. 20, f. 13, 1878.

Shell acutely pyramidal-turreted, thin, polished ; spire subulate-attenuated, ending in a nucleus of two very small rotund turns. Whorls fifteen, the posterior ones flat, the anterior ones slightly convex ; ornamented by three inconspicuous (sometimes obsolete) spiral threads, which are equidistant from each other and from the sutures, the interstices faintly spirally striated ; a shallow sulcus separates the anterior thread from the medial one ; incremental lines deeply flexuous, hardly visible.

Aperture subquadrangular, base finely concentrically lined. Length, 13 ; width, 3·75.

Localities.—Eocene : Muddy Creek *(Tenison-Woods.')*; River Murray Cliffs !; Gellibrand River !; Fyansford !; Mornington !.

T. platyspira resembles *T. congelata*, Ads. & Reeve, but that shell seems to be wanting in the deep sigmoidal growth-lines.

GENUS MESALIA.

Mesalia stylacris, *spec. nov.* Pl. ix., fig. 2.

Shell minute, thin, and pyramidally turreted, with a mucronate apex ; pullus cylindric of four narrow convex whorls ; spire-whorls five, convex or subangulated medially, ornamented by about seven narrow flat threads ; body-whorl convex to the rounded or subangulated periphery ; lirate and crossed by slightly sigmoidal incremental striæ ; base flattened or subconvex ; aperture oval ; outer lip thin, medially ecurved ; columella thick, arched, flattened, and margined at the exterior, callously united to the outer lip.

Dimensions.—Length, 4 ; breadth, 2 (vix.).

Locality.—Eocene : "Turritella-banks," Blanche Point, Aldinga Cliffs (common !).

This diminutive species of the genus is otherwise distinguished by its styliform apex.

FAMILY VERMETIDÆ.

GENUS THYLACODES.

Shell adherent, irregularly twisted, without laminæ or keels internal, but frequently concamerated.

SYNOPSIS OF SPECIES.

Posteriorly compactly coiled, afterwards lengthened.
Whorls embracing forming a broad cone. 1. *actinotus.*
Whorls contiguous forming a cylinder.
Surface lirate and finely costate. 2. *cratericulus.*
Surface roundly costate. 3. *conohelix.*
Posteriorly irregularly and loosely coiled.
Uncoiled portion much extended, densely squamosely ribbed.
4. *asper*
Uncoiled portion short : distantly ribbed. 5. *rudis.*
Shell vermiculate, slender, finely sculptured. 6. *Adelaidensis.*

1. Thylacodes actinotus, *spec. nov.* Pl. ix., fig. 1.

Solitary or rarely two together ; whorls embracing and reciprocally adherent except the last turn, which is extended into a very short erect tube. The aggregate mass is broadly conical : ornamented with thin lamellose radial ridge ; the free tubular portion circular in section.

Dimensions.—Diameters, 5 to 6 : height (ex. free tube), 2·5.

Locality.—Eocene : Adelaide-bore !.

2. Thylacodes cratericulus, *spec. nov.* Pl. ix., fig. 3.

Solitary or two together, early whorls irregularly coiled, anterior whorls compacted, irregularly conoid or shortly cylindroid, finally obliquely-extended into a long much-narrowed tube. Whorls ornamented with five or six spiral ridges crossed by straight threads producing square or oblong fenestrations : basal part of tube similarly ornamented gradually becoming obsolete towards the extremity.

Dimensions.—Diameters of base, 6·5 and 5·5 ; length of tube, 8 : its diameter, 1·5.

Localities. -Eocene : Muddy Creek ! : Mornington ! ; Fyansford ! : Gellibrand River !.

3. Thylacodes conohelix, *Ten.-Woods.* Pl. ix., fig. 11.

Vermetus conohelix, Tenison-Woods, Proc. Roy. Soc. Tasm. for 1876, p. 100, 1877.

Solitary, "tube adhering, corrugated, coiled ; lower whorls laterally depressed into a ridge, and coiled upon each other with a truncated flattened hollow cone of two whorls, at the apex the tube becomes free, obliquely erect, flexuous, and cylindrical ; aperture somewhat thick and orbicular. Height of cone, 3 ; breadth, 6 ; length of free end, 5 ; width of aperture, 1."

The common form of this shell at Spring Creek, which I figure, has a more contracted base, and the anterior whorls forming a cylinder.

Localities. — Table Cape *(Ten.-Woods.!)* : Spring Creek (common !); Moorabool Valley, and Bellarine Peninsula *(G. B. Pritchard.!)*.

4. Thylacodes asper, *spec. nov.* Pl. ix., fig. 10.

Solitary, early whorls more or less regularly convolute ; finally horizontally extended, at first attached, but largely free. Free tube with crowded, slightly elevated longitudinal ribs, narrower than the sulci, crossed by intricately-disposed lamellar threads, which produce asperities on the ribs.

Dimensions.—Diameter of the close spiral, 6 ; of free tube, 3·5.

Locality.—Eocene: Gellibrand River !.

5. Thylacodes rudis, *spec. nov.* Pl. ix., fig. 8.

Usually solitary ; base contortedly coiled, broadly and laterally attached ; anterior whorls rounded, more loosely coiled and irregularly bent, free part of tube short, not contracted, circular in section. The early whorls are concamerated. Surface ornamented with longitudinal liræ, about eleven on upper and lateral areas, distantly squamosely elevated.

Dimensions.—Diameter of aggregate mass, about 25; diameter of tube, 5·5 to 6.

Locality.—Eocene : Table Cape !, Gellibrand River !.

This species is the fossil analogue of *Vermetus arenarius*, Quoy and Gaimard, from which it differs by less-compactly-coiled and abruptly-bent whorls, and fewness of longitudinal liræ.

6. Thylacodes Adelaidensis, *spec. nov.* Pl. ix., fig. 9.

Solitary. Attached portion not known. Free part filiform, irregularly bent, circular in section ; surface ornamented with slender, obtuse threads, about 25 at the widest part (sometimes obsolete), minutely squamosely elevated at the intercrossing of regular circumscribing striæ.

Dimensions.—Known only by fragments, the greatest diameter of which is 2·5 ; diameter at the only partition observed, 1.

Localities.—Eocene : Adelaide bore and "Turritella-beds," Aldinga Cliffs.

This species closely resembles in size and form *V. anguillinus*, Desh., of the Parisian Eocene, with actual specimens of which I have made comparison, but differs from it by more distant threads.

EPPLANATION TO PLATES VI. TO X.

N.B.—The figures are of the natural size, except when otherwise stated.

PLATE VI.

Fig.
1. Natica sub-Noæ, *Tate*. Spring Creek, 2×.
2. Natica varians, *Tate*. Muddy Creek.
3. Natica substolida, *Tate*. Muddy Creek.
4. Natica gibbosa, *Hutton*. Murray Desert.
5. Natica Mooraboolensis, *Tate*. Moorabool River.
6. Natica subinfundibulum, *Tate*. Muddy Creek.
7. Natica balteatella, *Tate*. Pliocene : Dry Creek-bore.
8. Natica subvarians, *Tate*. Aldinga Cliffs.
9. Natica varians, *Tate*. Muddy Creek.
10. Natica subvarians, *Tate*. Gippsland.

PLATE VII.

Fig.
1. Calyptraea subtabulata, *Tate*. Table Cape.
2. Calyptraea crassa, *Tate*. Gippsland.
3. Calyptraea undulata, *Tate*. Muddy Creek.
4. Calyptraea placuna, *Tate*. Adelaide-bore.
5. Heligmope Dennanti, *Tate*. Muddy Creek.
6. Calyptraea corrugata, *Tate*. Muddy Creek.
7. A young individual variation of *C. crassa*.
8. Capulus circinatus, *Tate*. Adelaide-bore.
9. Calyptropsis arachnoideus, *Tate*. Adelaide-bore.
10. Sigaretus microstira, *Tate*. Spring Creek.

PLATE VIII.

Fig.
1. Turritella Aldingæ, *Tate*. Adelaide-bore.
2. Turritella Warburtoni, *Ten.-Woods*. Table Cape.
3. Turritella Murrayana, *Tate*. River Murray Cliffs.
4. Turritella acricula, *Tate*. River Murray Cliffs.
5. Turritella septifraga, *Tate*. Spring Creek.
6. Turritella Sturtii, *Ten.-Woods*. Table Cape.
7. Turritella conspicabilis, *Tate*. Gippsland.
8. Turritella tristira, *Tate*, var. Gippsland.
9. Turritella platyspira, *Ten.-Woods*. Muddy Creek.
10. Turritella pagodula, *Tate*. Gippsland.
11. Turritella gemmulata, *Tate*. Muddy Creek.

PLATE IX.

Fig.
1. Thylacodes actinotus, *Tate*. Adelaide-bore.
2. Mesalia stylacris, *Tate*. Aldinga.
3. Thylacodes cratericulus, *Tate*. Mornington.
4. Turritella acricula, *Tate*, var. Gellibrand River.
5. Crepidula dubitabilis, *Tate*. Gippsland.
6. Turritella conspicabilis, *Tate*, var. Spring Creek.
7. Turritella acricula, *Tate*, var. Gippsland.
8. Thylacodes rudis, *Tate*. Table Cape.
9. Thylacodes Adelaidensis, *Tate*. Adelaide-bore.
10. Thylacodes asper, *Tate*. Gellibrand River.
11. Thylacodes conohelix, *Tenison-Woods*. Spring Creek.
12. Turritella acricula, *Tate*, var. Table Cape.

PLATE X.

Fig.
1. Scalaria leptalea, *Tate*. Camperdown. Enlarged 5x., and magnified apex.
2. Euspira effusa. *Tate*. Adelaide-bore. Dorsal aspect and magnified portion of surface ; 2a. Aperture of another specimen.
3. Turritella tristira, *Tate*. Table Cape. Nat. size and magnified portion of surface.
4. Natica limata, *Tate*. Muddy Creek. Nat. size and portion of surface enlarged.
5. Natica Aldingensis, *Tate*. Adelaide-bore. (The carination is due to fracture in life.)
6. Natica Hamiltonensis, *Tate*. Muddy Creek.
7. Natica perspectiva, *Tate*. Muddy Creek. Enlarged 1·5x.
8. Natica arata, *Tate*. River Murray Cliffs.
9. Natica vixumbilicata, *Ten.-Woods* Table Cape.
10. Crossea semiornata, *Tate*. Spring Creek. Nat. size and portion of penultimate whorl enlarged.
11. Natica subinfundibulum, *Tate*. Muddy Creek. (Figures not correctly drawn.)

www.ingramcontent.com/pod-product-compliance
Lightning Source LLC
Chambersburg PA
CBHW021609270326

41931CB00009B/1398